In Retrospect

Things I Treasured

Doris Butz

ISBN 978-1-60920-147-0
Printed in the United States of America

© 2022 Doris Butz
All rights reserved

Library of Congress-in-Publication Data

API
Ajoyin Publishing, Inc.
P.O. Box 342
Three Rivers, MI 49093
www.ajoyin.com

No part of this book may be reproduced or transmitted in any form or by any means, electronic or mechanical—including photocopying, recording, or by any information storage and retrieval system—without permission in writing from the author, except as provided by United States of America copyright law.

Please direct your inquiries to admin@ajoyin.com

TABLE OF CONTENTS

Doris Butz: 4/29/70 1
Korea 3
Not Yet 5
Mommy Had a Ritual 6
Tea Parties 11
Celebration of Life 12
The Visit 13
Fishin' Gone 14
For These Things I Am Thankful 15
Her Angel 17
A Valentine to My Class 18
December 26, 1983 (Monday) 20
January 16, 1984 (Monday) 21
February 15, 1984 (Sunday) 23
February 12, 1984 (Sunday) 24
February 15, 1984 (Wednesday) 25
A Letter to God 26
Another Letter to God 27
A Letter to God 28
A Letter to God 29
Written for Carol: As Her Children Leave the Nest 30
To Bob: Memorial Day 1984 32
A Letter to God Sunday 1992 34
And Another Letter to God November 30, 1992 36
October 31, 1993 (Sunday) 37
A Letter to God July 9, 1995 38
Austin 39
Colors 40

In Retrospect: Things I Treasured

Doris Butz
4/29/70

There was a time when in my youth, I dreamed the dreams of all young girls.

A knight in shining armor would appear from Westward bringing pearls.

He'd lure me onto handsome steed and carry me to castle fair.

Where we would live forevermore, relaxed and happy dwelling there.

But days crept by becoming years, and childish dreams were put away.

Life soon became a ritual with lots more work and much less play.

I met a man and fell in love, one day to be his blushing bride.

Not thinking of my dreams of yore, working
proudly by his side.

Now hairs of gray are creeping in
and sight improved, for now I see.

This knight in shining armor did, appear
from west and marry me.

His mighty steed a light blue Ford, both
pearls and diamonds were his lure.

Our castle was a lovely place, three rooms
upon the second floor.

How grateful now I am to God, for
giving me this sight within.

My wildest hopes and dreams fulfilled, I love
this man. Thank God, Amen.

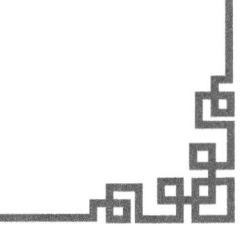

In Retrospect: Things I Treasured

Korea

The grass is green upon that hill
and flowers grow where children play.

It wasn't always quiet there in that strange
land so far away.

My mind is clear remembering headlines
printed for all to see.

The "Big War" ended five years ago, a new
War is about to be.

The reasons repeat with each new war
"I need your land," and "You're to blame."

"I'll gather my friends and you shall see,
your land will soon go up in flame."

Doris Butz

On that hill so far away men came together
Face-to-face.

They killed and maimed each other there
and scarred and stained that far off place.

The names and faces of these brave
men are forgotten to all but their next of kin.

The reasons they fought and their sufferings, too,
Are lost to the likes of me and you.

Now see the grass that's growing there
and watch the children run and play.

Do you suppose that we have learned,
or will we fight another day?

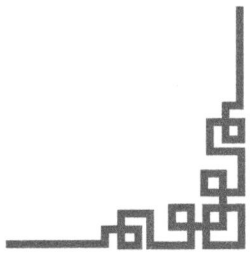

In Retrospect: Things I Treasured

Time marches on down that slippery slope,
Our work is still there and so is our hope.
Towel in hand and dishes still wet,
I guess I'm not through, at least not yet.

Grandchildren come in with arms open wide,
My joy at seeing them impossible to hide.
Hugs and kisses reveal a diaper that's wet,
I guess I'm not through, at least not yet.

Hungry mouths soon open wide for a spoon.
Mealtime again, it seems almost too soon.
Dishes to clear, a sink full all wet.
I guess I'm not through, at least not yet.

Bath time is over, children snuggle so near,
"Sing Jesus Loves Me please, Grandma, dear."
Wet towels abound, bathroom floor soaking wet.
I guess I'm not through, at least not yet.

I crawl into bed a smile on my face,
Thoughtful to God for all of this place.
I may be old and more likely to set,
But God says hold on, I'm not through with you yet!

Doris Butz

Mommy Had a Ritual

Mommy had a ritual (I called her Mommy then).
She was the great "dust buster" cleaning house
From stern to stem.

Each special day and season, too,
She brought her bucket out.
And worked off all her worries,
Never did just sit and pout.

I was four and much too young,
To know that times were tough.
Dad's birthday came, depression ruled,
we barely had enough.

Mom got out her bucket to scrub the kitchen floor,
The room smelled like chocolate cake,
Her gift…
There'd be no more.

She planned to clean most everything,
Then set the kitchen table.
And wash her face and comb her hair,
To smile if she was able.

In Retrospect: Things I Treasured

"Puleeese," my brother and I jumped
Up and down and cried.
Fire whistles signaled excitement
We would not be denied.

The whistle count told all the kids,
Where the fire would be,
Two blocks away at the top of the hill
Was the spot where we could see.

The air was cold, we bundled up,
And trotted down the street.
While Sis our teenage supervisor,
Was leader of our fleet.

We stopped at every corner,
Obeying all the rules,
That boys and girls were quick to learn,
Attending public schools.

The wind was brisk from our vantage point,
The crest of Canterbury Hill.
A smoky spire in the meadowland,
Soon lost us to the chill.

Doris Butz

The road was steep up that mighty hill,
One of our favorite places.
When the snow was deep, our sleds
Would line up there for races.

I clasped our supervisor's coat
and trailed along behind.
The other kids stepped off the
curb and crossed the street just fine.

Sis and I came right along,
Bringing up the rear.
We laughed and shivered as we ran,
Never a sign of fear.

The driver did not see us,
As he came across the hill.
The car was old, sun in his face,
This would not be his will.

The impact threw me far and wide,
My sitters coat was torn.
I held on tight with all my might,
The other's youth was shorn.

In Retrospect: Things I Treasured

Time marched on and I recovered,
The doctor came, removed the cast.
Months of lying flat were over,
and now I would be free at last.

My legs were weak and thin and brown,
I was afraid I could not walk.
The doctor left, Mom saw him out,
And then came back to me to talk.

"You'll soon be strong enough to run
Outside to play."
"Just try," she said, as she left my room,
"I have work, you'll be okay."

The fears had hung around me,
Since that day so long ago,
When doctors told my mother,
"She'll never walk you know."

They echoed in my childish mind,
As I stood and held the wall.
And inched along up to the door,
I gave the task my all.

Doris Butz

I peered around the corner,
As pleased, as I could be!
All fear had flown away,
Cause Mommy I could see.

She was in the kitchen
Down on her knees again,
Scrubbing, praying, planning,
Life was sweet, amen!

In Retrospect: Things I Treasured

Tea Parties

Mom,

Tea parties at my little gray table, chairs pulled close, real tea (pretty weak) and sugar in the tiny china sugar bowl. How patient you were to play with me. White organdy bedspreads, handmade with lots of ruffles. A pile of pretty ribbons, all washed and ironed, ready to tie on my braids. Doll's dresses that matched my own. Underpants made to match my dresses. A kitchen that smelled of homemade bread and rice pudding. Singing canaries, and you and I laughing, dancing to the latest polka tune.

It's such fun to walk down memory lane with you. We were good friends. The times I am most thankful for are the ones you'd probably call "hard times." You were short of money but had lots of ideas and time and love. We even jumped rope together.

Thanks, Mom, for a lifetime of love.

Doris Butz

Celebration of Life

When life is over and days are done,
We'll each be judged by God's own Son.

And at that time, He'll surely see,
The fruits beneath our lifelong tree.

He'll pick them up, inspect them 'round,
For each a jewel goes in our crown.

The 80 years, just now complete,
When spread before the Master's feet.

Are bound to fill your crown of gold,
Complete with precious jewels, I'm told.

Friends and family, even now can see,
The fruit beneath your…lifelong tree.

In Retrospect: Things I Treasured

The Visit

My life is blessed with many things. One is when my telephone rings and a voice announces, "I'll be there soon, maybe Friday, just about noon." I spread the news and the family cheer, it won't be long, and she'll be here.

I put clean sheets on her bed and thaw out the meat. Our visits may be short, but it's always so sweet. The arrival brings lots of hugs and kisses, we continue our talk, and a beat never misses. It continues as though we were tied at the heart, always in tune and never apart.

A couple of days sharing breakfast, lunch and dinner, and a snack before bed. (We are not getting thinner.)

We laugh and have fun, and to tell you the truth, I can't wait for the next visit from my dear friend Ruth.

Doris Butz

Fishin' Gone

I hadn't fished for years and lamented wasted time.
Closed eyes produced the visions of sun and wetted line.

I longed for days gone by when fishing with my Dad,
Produced the finest days a person ever had.

I bought myself a fishing pole and a dandy little kit.
Complete with reel and line and lures tucked inside of it.

I stashed it in my auto trunk with plans to get my license.
Then read the DNR fishing guide and came right to my senses.

I'd have to take a special course to attempt to understand,
The rules and regulations promulgated by this clan.

The exceptions and the references caused my head to spin around,
Even after reading it, I'm not sure what I found.

I have finally concluded that I'll give my gear away.
To some child without the money to buy some toys for play.

D. Butz
1993

In Retrospect: Things I Treasured

For These Things I Am Thankful

Thursday, November 27, 1997
Thanksgiving Day

Some things are hard to see,
Unless they are happening to me.
A cool breeze on a summer day,
A book to read, a game to play.
For these things I am thankful.

Some things are hard to see,
Unless they're happening to me.
My child's voice upon the phone,
Knowing I am not alone.
For these things I am thankful.

Some things are hard to see,
Unless they're happening to me.
A son who loves me as I am,
Watching him become a man.
For these things I am thankful.

Doris Butz

Some things are hard to see,
Unless they're happening to me.
My husband's touch as he passes by,
His arms around me when I cry.
For these things I am thankful.

Some things are hard to see,
Unless they're happening to me.
The joy of watching Kristen grow,
To see the love within her flow.
For these things I am thankful.

Some things are hard to see,
Unless they're happening to me.
Reflecting on times from yesterday,
Words of love those in my family say.
For these things I am thankful.

My mind is full as I grow old.
Of gifts of love, not gifts of gold.
Hard times always come and go,
But one thing I will always know…
For Jesus Christ, I am thankful.

Her Angel

There was a little girl who hated the dark and always wanted to sleep with her mom. One day, her great-grandma told her a story of an angel that used to visit her, but only when she was alone in her bed. The angel was beautiful and told her wonderful stories of Jesus.

Oh how the little girl wanted to talk to "her" angel. She tried to crawl in her own bed that night and be quiet, but soon went back to Grammy's bed. "Grammy, you said an angel might come if I waited in my own bed. And none came!"

"How long did you wait?" asked Gram. "Weeeelllll… not too long.." Gram said to try it again for the whole night.

That night as the little girl said her prayers, she asked God to send the angel so she could see her. After a while, she fell asleep, and the angel came and kissed her on her cheek. The angel was very pretty.

In the morning, Grammy said, "You're really blessed. Some people wait a lifetime for a kiss from an angel."

Doris Butz

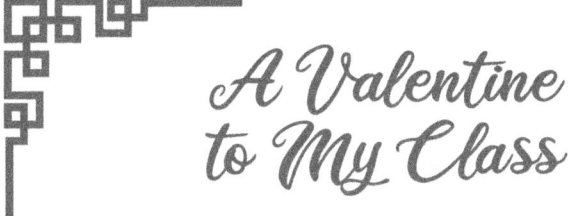
A Valentine to My Class

I'll be 74
in just a few days,
And finding it easier
To seek ones to praise.

Oh, I saw them before,
And their wonderful deeds
But I spoke not a word
Kept them planted like seeds.

Now that I'm old
And looking around
I see people leaving
Not knowing the sound.

Of words left unspoken
Words of love, life and pleasure.
Gifts of the moment,
With no lifetime to treasure.

Each person I met,
And some really knew.
Gave me a gift,
While passing life through.

In Retrospect: Things I Treasured

Maybe they smiled
Or held open a door,
Were they my role models
Giving memories to store?

Those with great brains or athletic talent,
Admired from afar with words kept silent.
The quiet ones not given to talk,
Not knowing who saw them, admiring their walk.

I want each to know,
What's now in my heart.
The unspoken words,
Before I depart.

The life, love, and joy
Spread back and forth
By each girl,
And by each boy.

I want you to see
How important you've been.
To all of your classmates
Especially me.

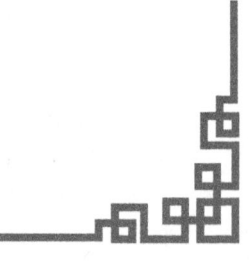

Doris Butz

December 26, 1983
Monday

Beginnings and endings are difficult, each one forged from fear. Today we ended a relationship of 15 years. Our beloved companion and faithful friend Holly had a stroke and had to be put to sleep.

I was afraid for her, and for myself. I didn't want her to know any pain and I didn't want her to feel betrayed by me. Randy was with me. Bob prepared her grave beneath the beautiful fruit trees in the orchard.

It will be a long time until I stop listening for her and waiting for her greeting at the end of the day.

I know of no Bible verse for comfort and cannot be sure of where dog souls go. Yet, my God speaks of a day when lions shall lay down with lambs, so I must conclude that animals will be present after His second coming. Hurrah!! Holly won't be left behind!

In Retrospect: Things I Treasured

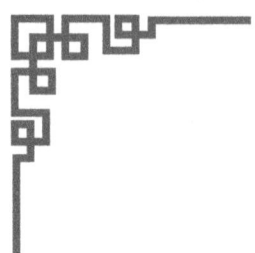

January 16, 1984
Monday

My God is the motivating force in my life. He is wonderful, and I find Him in those around me. My granddaughter Kristen was with me this weekend, a constant reminder of a God who keeps His promises.

Beulah spent all day Saturday here. I love her. She knitted a pair of booties for Kristen while we chatted. She is remarkable, 82 years young.

Her life reflects the love she has for God and is an example for all. She has shared some of her youthful experiences with me, brought up on a farm with a sister and brother younger than she.

She worked the farm along with her parents. Berries or cucumbers were picked each day when in season. Her mom worked the fields until 4:30 PM on Saturday. She still had her housecleaning and baking to do.

Doris Butz

Beulah's dad made it a practice to ask the visiting pastor home to dinner on Sunday, so an unknown number were to be fed, maybe 10 people. Beulah helped her mom.
She spoke of buttermilk biscuits, the highest she ever saw, made with the top milk and real butter, browned to perfection, split and then covered with chicken gravy that had egg yolks in it. Never was one leftover.
I hope she continues to share her experiences with me. She silently witnesses that toil and hardships should not be spoken of with a resentful attitude but remembered as the training provided by God to mold us into that which He desires. He fashioned her into a lovely masterpiece.

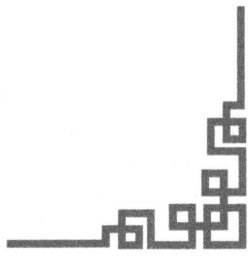

February 15, 1984
Sunday

I have been diligently searching for God's will in my life. Like most of the people around me, I am searching for an instant answer. Add two cups of water, stir, process in the microwave and *Boom*! An instant answer.

I am beginning to realize that I may never have what the world would call an answer. The end may be the process.

I have felt led by God to feed patients three days a week at Fairview. I rolled it around in my mind for some time and finally decided I must step forward to try to follow the Spirit's gentle leading. He never pushes me, just gently nudges, and then steps back to wait for my response.

This time I responded quickly, and I find that I am benefitting more than those infirm. I rejoice in a simple sign of progress in Ruth or a smile from a normally depressed and aged patient. Today, I must respond again to His gentle leading.

He cannot fully use me when I am not actively involved in a church. Somewhere along the way, I became disenchanted with structured churches. They have too many politics involved in their leadership and not enough deep, committed love and worship of Him.

I must resign myself to the fact that it still is His church and although now imperfect, one day the Bride will be ready. I must be part of the preparation for the wedding, striving to do His bidding.

Doris Butz

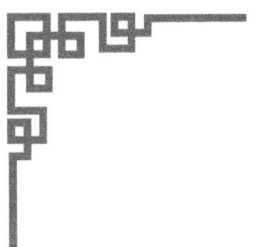

February 12, 1984
Sunday

Another ending and beginning. Forty-nine years old. I dislike being the center of attention and family and office celebrations make me squirm. However, as birthdays go, this was one of the great ones.

Sharon and Kristen joined me at work on Friday and I had lunch with all of the girls. I really appreciated their effort. And on Saturday, Bob and I had a whole day together shopping and going to a museum. Today, we had a family dinner at Mom's. If they continue to behave in this manner, I will be too spoiled to live with.

Thank you, God, for a wonderful family. I love them so much.

February 15, 1984
Wednesday

This morning while driving to work, I thought about how much You mean to me. There are times when I love You more than life. When I am away from you, there is an empty place in my heart and life that no other one could ever fill.

Those very special times when You and I are alone and communicating in an intimate way sends my spirit soaring and gives me renewed energy.

I am thankful that You are always there when I am overcome by sadness. I love You, honor You and trust You. You are my life, my friend and my all.

I only wish to be totally Yours, my precious Lord.

Doris Butz

A Letter to God

Lord, it's not so much fun looking into a mirror and seeing a once young face and body sagging and wrinkling with age.

It would be easy to be depressed, especially now, Lord, when youth worshipping is in fashion.

Help me, Lord, to focus on all those wonderful gifts that You present only as age increases. A beautiful granddaughter, my children growing in wisdom and in love for You, a husband content to be by my side and an increased personal love and knowledge of You.

Help me, Lord, when I look into the mirror to see Your gifts.

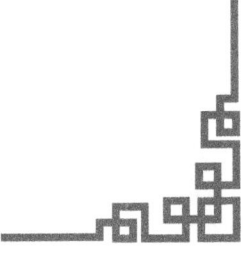

Another Letter to God

I thank you, Father, for opening my eyes and heart to Your chosen people. Each year, I learn more about them, and knowing more about them is knowing more about You.

Help me, Lord, to remember Jesus was and still is a Jew.

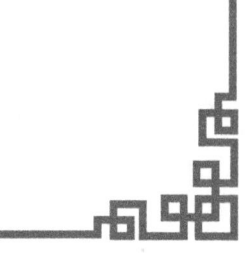

Doris Butz

A Letter to God

Someone made reference to another person as, "You know the kind of a person who just has to be needed?" It is wrong, Lord, to want to be needed? Or am I confusing wanting to be needed with joy in helping?

I get such a thrill in doing the unexpected. I apologized to a child after a collision in a store. He was sure he was about to be scolded. I get such joy from seeing the faces of the patients at Fairview when they know someone cares. I feel better if I can cook a casserole for a person who is hurting or mourning. I don't want to be a "glory seeker," Lord.
Help me to keep my eyes focused on You in each of these people.

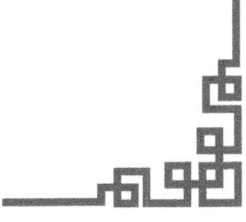

In Retrospect: Things I Treasured

A Letter to God

I'm still praying, Lord, for Your direction in my life, waiting for the big answer. I don't know what makes me think my demands and cries should be immediately answered.
Who am I, that I should have such preferred treatment?

It would be a well-traveled road, if everyone could be positive that a simple *yes* to God would result in the delivery of a clearly-marked road map. Maybe it's the other way around.

A step at a time into the dark. No map, no clear definition in the trail, just You as a lamp by my side, giving only enough light for the next step into the unknown.

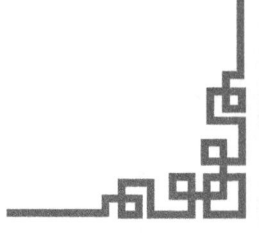

Doris Butz

Written for Carol:

As Her Children Leave the Nest.

I've been building ships almost all my life. Oh, I have been employed at other jobs at the same time, but I've always been working on my ships.

Carefully, I've carved and fitted each piece with loving care. I have them just about completed now, Lord. They are filled with all the things I thought would be helpful on a long journey. The tide is ready and impatient for the launching and yet there is still some polishing I'd like to complete.

I'm thankful, Father, for the extra time You gave me to work on them. So many others have launched ships before they were seaworthy.

Why, as the task is completed, is there such sadness? What does a shipbuilder do when it is too late to start another ship?

In Retrospect: Things I Treasured

You taught me a lot about them over the years, Lord, and now as this life's work is completed, I see even more clearly what is needed to promote the building of sound ships strong enough to withstand stormy seas.

Here I am, Lord, trying to have the courage to smile while my beloved ships sail away. I have my tools ready and they're still sharp.

Maybe I will no longer build ships myself, but I could help another builder! Spread a new set of blueprints before me, Lord.

Help me to be patient while You explain Your plans.

Doris Butz

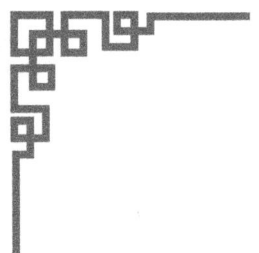

To Bob:

Memorial Day
1984

He churns and boils deep inside, from things once born of family pride.

Foundations laid long before he even opened earthy door.

"Accomplish something throughout life, no matter that it causes strife!

A man is measured by his work, of tasks complete, no duty shirk."

Now years have gone and shoulders bend, from toiling days without an end.

A restlessness begins to show from where it came he'll never know.

He didn't take the time to see, that life begins in eternity.

A journey that cannot begin without forgiveness for all sin.

Hand in hand with Christ the King, talking, reading, studying.

Spending time with Him whose love, extends into the heaven above.

And cultivating Christian friend, who'll be our neighbor in the end.

On his tombstone they'll surely write: "He labored hard both day and night."

I wish that it would rather read:
> "He left upon this earth a seed, of love and joy and kindly word, told when needed to be heard. Scattered everywhere he'd go, left to blossom and to grow."

Doris Butz

A Letter to God

Sunday 1992

Time has flown, Lord. Days are crammed with pressing needs. I haven't taken the time to write to You in a long time. Even though we relate daily, it's not the same as a written word.

We have moved into the lovely home You gave us and have been working every day to paint and repair it. Planning to retire in a little over a year without pressing financial needs has kept us busy.

Our precious Kristen is beautiful, and I ask for your continued protection and leadership in her life. I can't believe she is 10 years old already. She's a good student and the first female athlete in our family. Thank you for letting me play an important role in her life. Of all your wonderful gifts, this is the most rewarding.

Many things have happened since 1984. I have been promoted at work, and without Your daily gifts of wisdom, patience and love, I could not do this work. Your basic training in dealing with hard times in life helps me to extend a hand in love to those I contact each day.

Bob has had two surgeries, one while in the Reserves. You miraculously brought him through a ruptured intestine. That's a wonderful story of Your love to be recorded at a later time. And he is now recovering from a hernia operation.

Dad is failing and can't weigh a hundred pounds. Most of the time we are unable to rouse him. Mom is so faithful to provide him with around-the-clock care. Your gift of strength allows this precious 78-year-old to remain strong. Bless her, Lord…

I find myself very weary, Lord. I need some of Your renewing of my strength that I may spiritually soar with eagles. I hit a deer the other day on the way to work. I can still close my eyes and hear the two thuds and see her slide across the hood, hit the windshield and slide off the roof next to my door. Thank you, Father, for providing me with a guardian angel. Not even a dent in the car, and I wasn't showered with glass. The car and I are both intact.

Thank you for the one scratch on the glass as proof that this really did happen and isn't some "fish" story.

Doris Butz

And Another Letter to God

November 30, 1992

Bob and I watched Billy Graham tonight on TV. I thank you for him, Lord, and for all of his team. His message has always been the same simple presentation of salvation, each time presented with a fascinating magnetism. The sound of his voice and the songs of George Beverly Shea remind me of Your faithfulness.

Those first few years of our marriage were so difficult for me. The flood, the loss of work, return to the Air Force, Bob's mom and her constant anger, Bobby's death and then my near-death experience. Thank you for bringing me to the realization that nothing has worth unless you are in it.

Through tears I pictured You. I listened to my old record player and George's songs of you over and over. Billy's crusades on TV held my fascination. You showed your steadfast love and used the same men to carry your message then as today.

They represent Your constancy. Thirty-six or thirty-seven years have passed, and You still love me, regardless of all my thoughts and deeds. That's miraculous.

I bow before you, Holy Father. I thank you for Your Son.

In Retrospect: Things I Treasured

Sunday
October 31, 1993

For years I've wondered why,
Dear Lord, did you place me here?

To work among the prisoners
Some people I should fear.

You know that I confess Your name,
Proclaiming You're my own,

Wouldn't it be kinder
To let me stay at home?

Some people get the easy road
Or so it seems from here,

But then, where is their reason,
To hold You VERY near?

Doris Butz

A Letter to God

July 9, 1995

Dear Lord,

I'm sorry for not writing sooner. I have been very lax. The reason I'm writing today? Joy!!

You know I've been thinking of my precious grandmother. To me, her name was Nana. How I loved and respected her. She was so quiet and gentle. She actually listened to me when I was a child.

Well, Mom came home today after visiting her sister and brought me words from Nana. Poems written long before!! A poem about Allen and me when we were five and three years old.

It was like talking to her, Lord. Thank You for seeing my need and filling it.

In Retrospect: Things I Treasured

Austin

He sat with his grandma
His great one, too.

We sat with Rebecca
No one ever knew.

One day childhood glances
Would grow to be,

A permanent place,
In a real family.

They grew up together
One household shared.

Led by a Momma
Who really cared.

Now each one is grown
Out of the house on their own.

Though paths led in separate ways,
They are together for all special days.

Doris Butz

Colors

Art is very important to me.
My palate is planned for eye to see.

Each color laid out in a special way,
Preparing for things I need to say.

Lots of white in large amounts
To temper the colors laid about.

Red is for anger hidden below,
The color on top just for show.

Blue is for sadness, placed to know
A spot we are often forced to go.

Black is always a place to hide,
Unending darkness deep inside.

Yellow is simply a softened spot.
A place to go before we depart.

Color your picture carefully,
Using white most generously.

Then, step aside to view
Your life of color painted by you.

www.ingramcontent.com/pod-product-compliance
Lightning Source LLC
Chambersburg PA
CBHW061346040426
42444CB00011B/3117